Praises Are Priceless

from, 'Life's Big Little Lessons'

Christine Merrell-Rawson

Dedication

<u>Inspired By</u>

Gary

Cory

Stephi

Nikki

Kiersten

Kyla

William

Forrest

&

Marcus

Acknowledgment

I must express my sincere gratitude to the friends and family members who made it possible to take this book from my personal journals and put it into the hands of you and your children and hopefully libraries around the world.

Tony Lowe

Rich and Lori Merrell

Gloria and Brett Krommenhoek

Marti Baldry Hooper

Keith Pitcock

Stan Norland

Lynn Merrell

Ralayne Buckley

Karen Ritchie

Tracey Tengs

Rena and Willy Downs

Tim and Rosemary Bean

Lori Conrath

Diane Marston

Dana and Mary Libby

Jessica & Gary Merrell

Page Blank Intentionally

Hi everyone, Phillip Praiser is my name.

Are you ready to read about where most praises come from?

Most praises come from within your HEART.

You don't have to be BIG or brave or smart.

Praises cheer people up throughout the day.

When you encourage them with the very words that you say.

Let's say mom just did something nice for you. Not only that but for your brother, too.

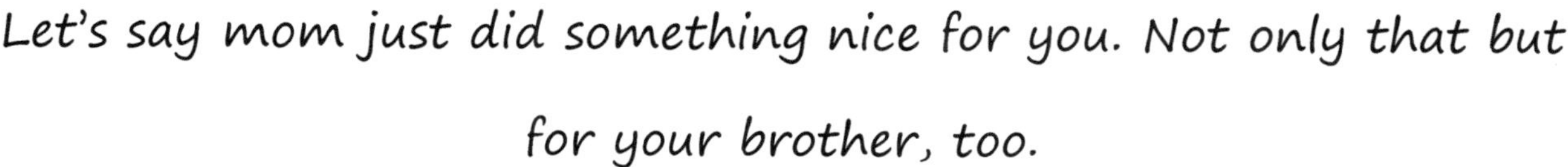

Well, now is the perfect time to smile and say...

"Hey, Mom, YOU just made our day!!!" That's what praise is.

your painting in art class today was amazing!
you're looking nice today, Mrs Rawsonz
You're the parents e

So, if we pay attention to all those around us, we'll begin to see

many a way...

To share a kind word and brighten up their day.

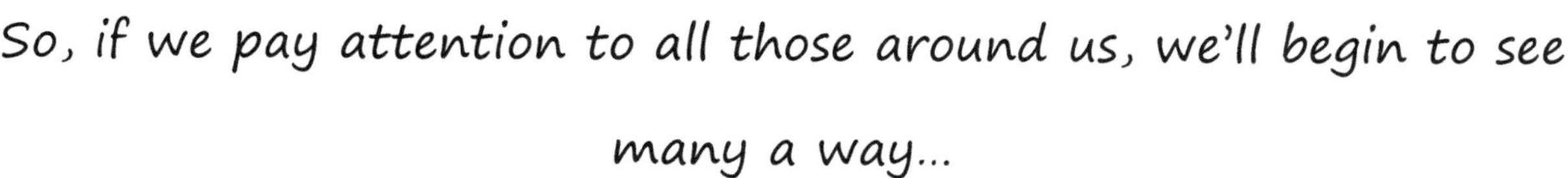

here, let me help you

What if you saw someone who is struggling or having a hard time?

How can you help them? Can you think of something kind to say? Something to build them up and brighten their day?

Maybe you have a friend who is feeling some doubt. They're finding it hard to figure something out.

Time to praise them!! Offer a clue that helps what is hard seem easier to do.

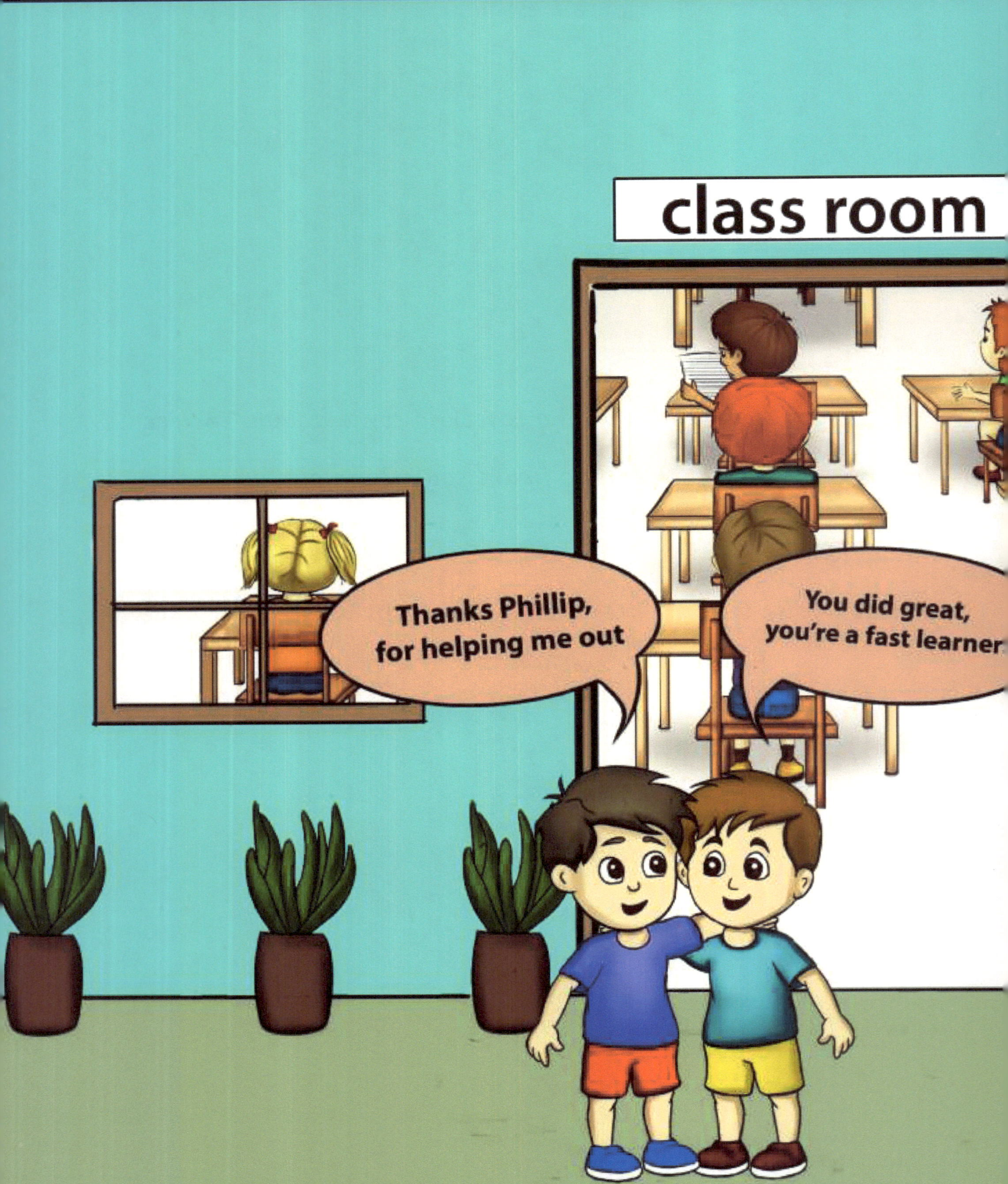

class room
Thanks Phillip, for helping me out
You did great, you're a fast learner

Then, PRAISE them again and point out what they did.

You'll help him or her feel like a really great kid!

Hey man thanks,
you just made my day

Don't be surprised if they turn to you and say, "Hey man,

THANKS! You just made MY day."

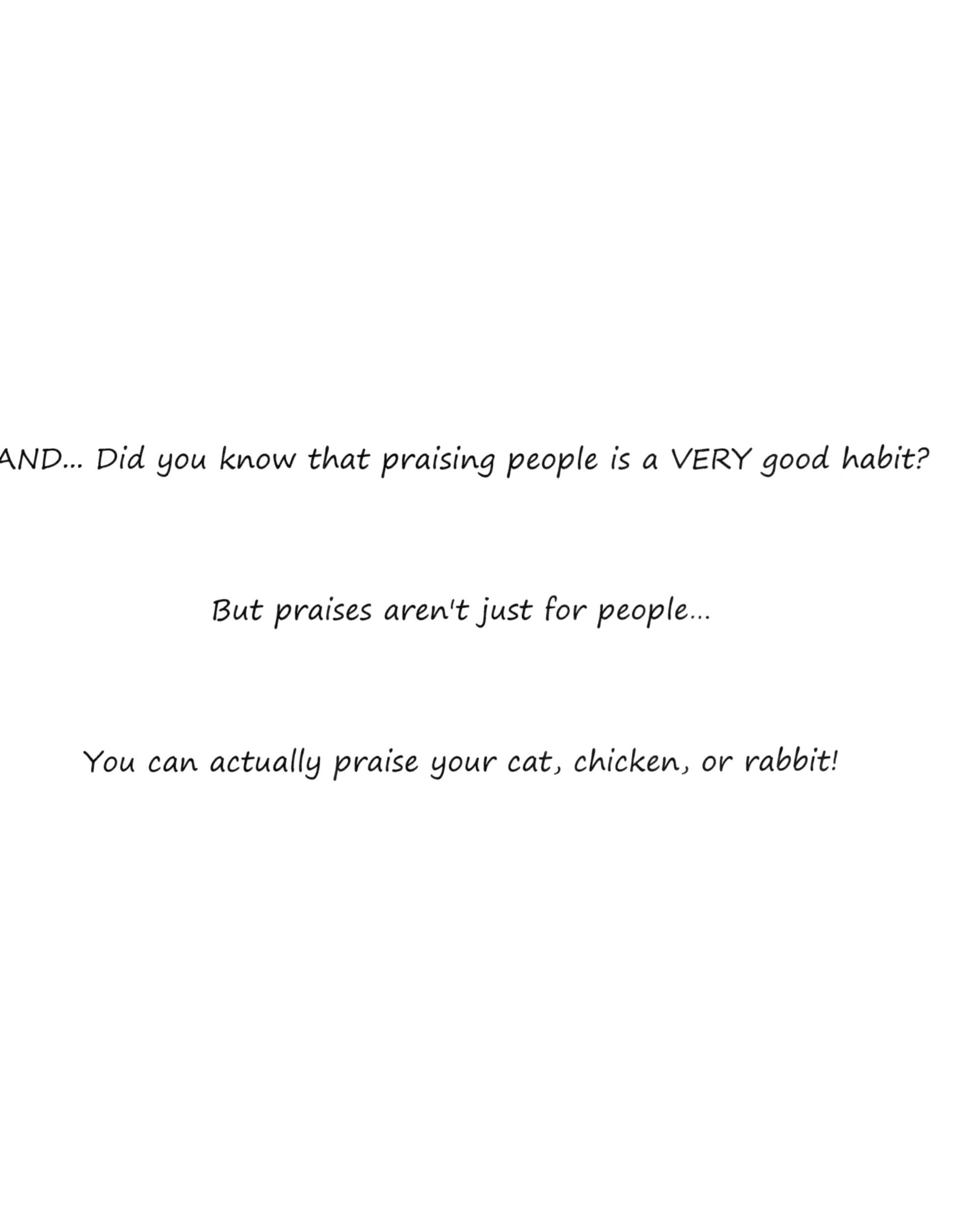

AND... Did you know that praising people is a VERY good habit?

But praises aren't just for people...

You can actually praise your cat, chicken, or rabbit!

So, try to remember each and every single day…

You can praise all living things with the very words that you say.

Don't ever forget...

The things you choose to say and the things you choose to do,

when done from the heart, will bring blessings back to YOU!!!

Praises are free, they don't cost a thing.

Praises are priceless, just watch the joy that they bring.

THE END

Let's talk about it

1. How do you feel when someone praises you?

2. How do you feel inside when you praise someone?

3. Whom did you praise today?